Check out all of the books in the Tell Me About Dinosaurs Series

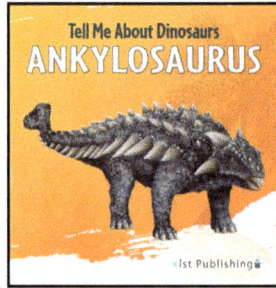

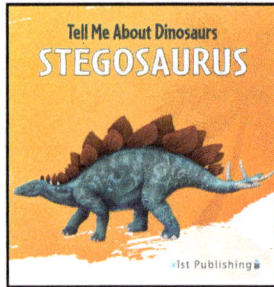

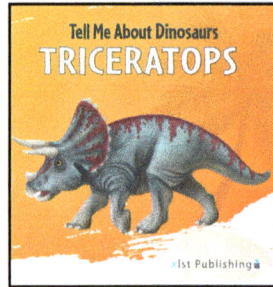

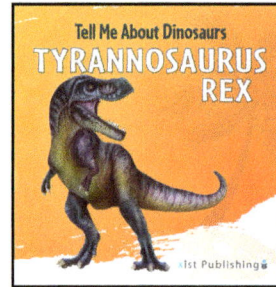

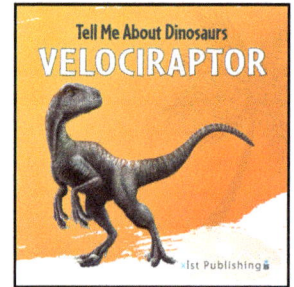

Tell Me About Dinosaurs
ANKYLOSAURUS
Xist Publishing

Tell Me About Dinosaurs
BRACHIOSAURUS
Xist Publishing

Tell Me About Dinosaurs
SPINOSAURUS
Xist Publishing

Tell Me About Dinosaurs
STEGOSAURUS
Xist Publishing

Tell Me About Dinosaurs
TRICERATOPS
Xist Publishing

Tell Me About Dinosaurs
TYRANNOSAURUS REX
Xist Publishing

Tell Me About Dinosaurs
VELOCIRAPTOR
Xist Publishing

Published in the United States by Xist Publishing
www.xistpublishing.com
© 2025 Copyright Xist Publishing

First Edition
Hardcover ISBN: 978-1-5324-5491-2
Paperback ISBN: 978-1-5324-5492-9
eISBN: 978-1-5324-5490-5

PUBLISHED IN TEXAS

Tell Me About Dinosaurs
BRACHIOSAURUS

Marjorie Seevers

Xist Publishing

Brachiosaurus was a very big dinosaur.

40 feet tall

85 feet long

4

It ate plants.

Brachiosaurus had a
long neck.

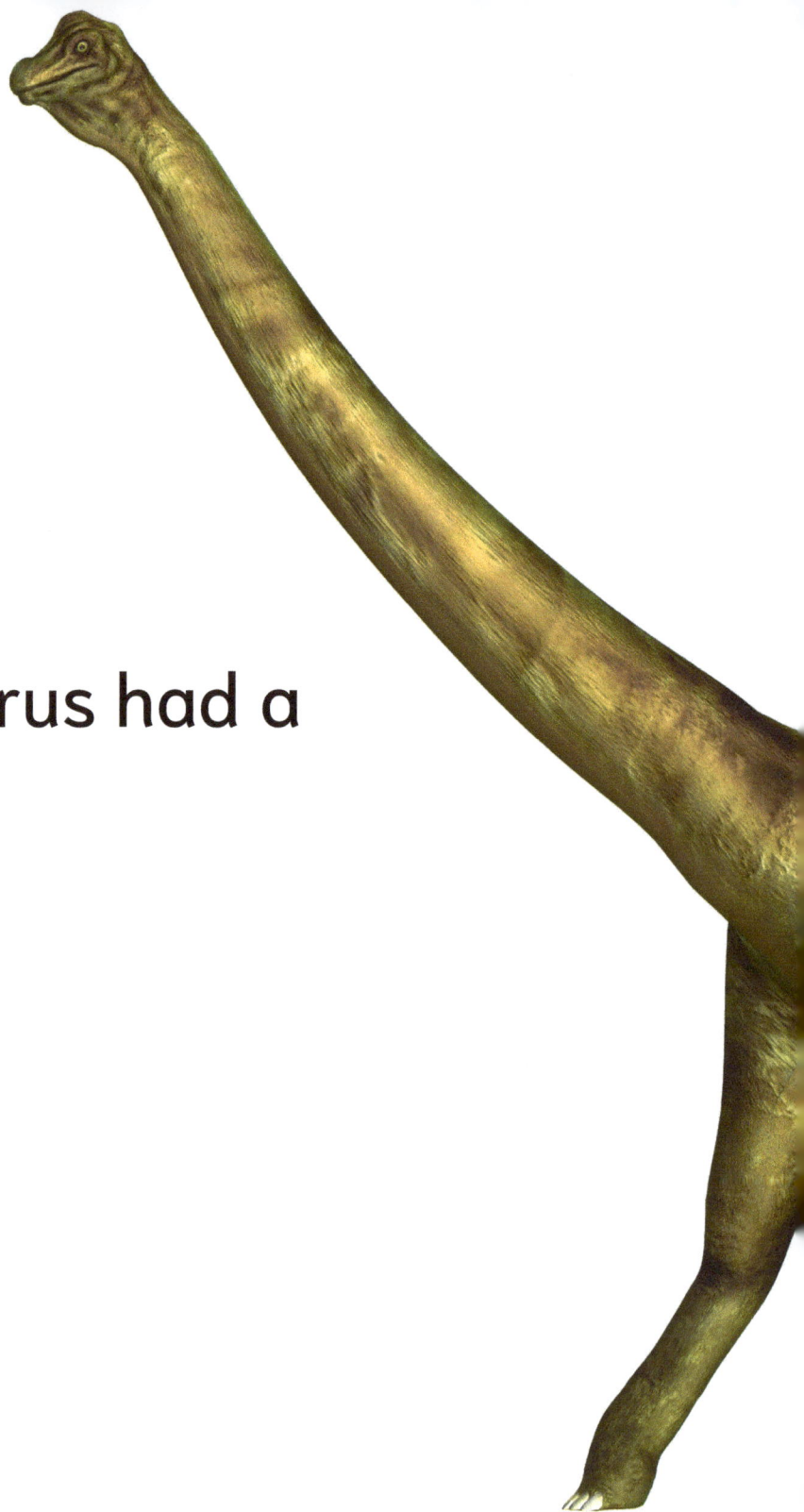

It could reach leaves in tall trees.

Brachiosaurus walked on four legs.

It had a very small head.

14

Brachiosaurus bones
are called fossils.

Which dinosaur is a Brachiosaurus?

What did Brachiosaurus eat?